PICTURE LIBR

CUSTOM

DUE DATE

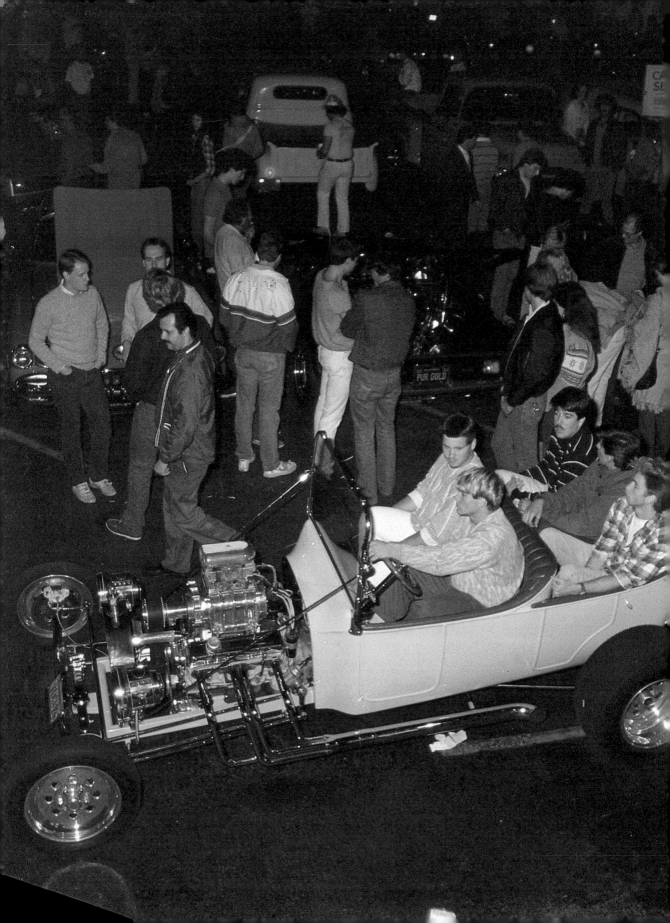

CUSTOM CARS

Norman Barrett

Franklin Watts

London   New York   Sydney   Toronto

First Paperback Edition 1990
ISBN 0-531-15177-8

© 1987 Franklin Watts Ltd

First published in Great Britain
    1987 by
Franklin Watts Ltd
12a Golden Square
London W1R 4BA

First published in the USA by
Franklin Watts Inc
387 Park Avenue South
New York
N.Y. 10016

First published in Australia by
Franklin Watts
14 Mars Road
Lane Cove
2066 NSW

UK ISBN: 0 86313 491 2
US ISBN: 0-531-10273-4
Library of Congress Catalog Card
Number 86-50639

Printed in Italy

Designed by
Barrett & Willard

Photographs by
Andy Willsheer
Street Machine Magazine

Illustration by
Rhoda & Robert Burns

Technical Consultant
Tony Beadle

Contents

Introduction	6
Custom car features	8
Street rods	10
Custom cars	13
Lowriders	18
Show cars	20
Vans and trucks	24
Kit cars	26
The story of custom cars	28
Facts and records	30
Glossary	31
Index	32

Introduction

Custom cars are cars that have been altered in some way to change their appearance. People who customize their cars do so to make them special, different from any other car.

Customizing might just involve fancy paintwork. But sometimes interiors and engines are also customized. A car may be changed or completely rebuilt.

△ This street rod illustrates all kinds of modifications. The chassis has been completely rebuilt, with flamed paintwork and an engine that is a work of art in itself.

Any kind of vehicle may be customized. "Street rods" are machines based on models originally made before 1949. Lowriders are a type of custom car in which the body has been considerably lowered.

Kit cars are special cars that can be bought in kit form and built up. Cars that are altered in such a way that they cannot be used on the road are called show cars.

△ The chosen theme for this car is obviously red, white and gleaming chrome. The theme extends to the interior and the engine.

Custom car features

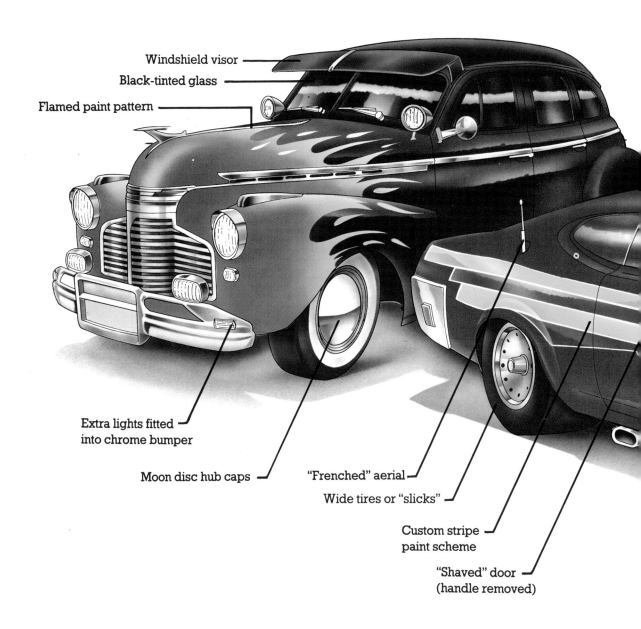

Windshield visor

Black-tinted glass

Flamed paint pattern

Extra lights fitted
into chrome bumper

Moon disc hub caps

"Frenched" aerial

Wide tires or "slicks"

Custom stripe
paint scheme

"Shaved" door
(handle removed)

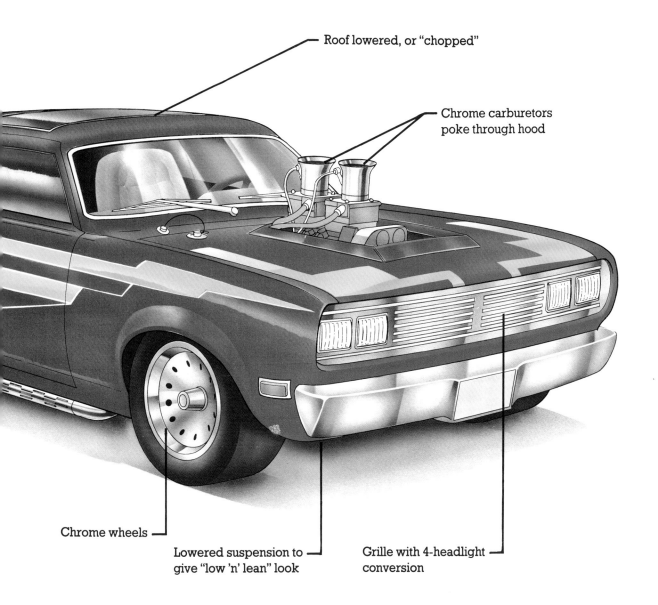

Roof lowered, or "chopped"

Chrome carburetors
poke through hood

Chrome wheels

Lowered suspension to
give "low 'n' lean" look

Grille with 4-headlight
conversion

Street rods

Old models are very popular. Street rods based on early cars are built up with body and chassis sections specially made for the purpose.

Street rods might look ancient, but they often include modern suspension, tires and engine parts for comfort, performance and smooth running.

▽ A 1933 Plymouth on an evening "cruise," in which street rods are shown off in the streets. "Chopping," the lowering of the roofline, is a popular customizing feature.

△ The body panels of this street rod have been reproduced based on a Model A roadster of the late 1920s. It has a "flathead" V-8 engine and whitewall tires of the 1940s.

▷ A close-up of the engine shows how much care is taken in every detail.

△ Street rods exhibited at a charity show. The one in front is based on a Model T Ford. The first of the mass-produced cars, Model Ts were built from 1909 to 1927. But they never had engines like this! The combination of fat rear wheels and smaller skinny ones at the front is called "big 'n' littles."

◁ Street rods can move, as this black roadster demonstrates.

Custom cars

There are no limits to what you can do to a car. If it is to be used on the road, however, it must conform with the laws of the highway.

Often, people customizing cars will choose a theme. This might be a color scheme or it might be based on a special subject. People may concentrate on the bodywork, the interior or the engine.

▽ This model has been chopped and lowered, and painted in eye-catching colors. Narrow chromed pipes that run along the side of a car below the body panels, like the exhaust here, are called "Lakes pipes." They give the car a lower, sleeker look.

◁ This extraordinary machine started life in 1976 as a Citroën CX. It has been almost completely rebuilt.

▷ The radiator grille, headlamps and paintwork are the strong features on this two-door sedan.

▽ This "stretched" VW limousine is made up of parts from seven different VWs.

◁ The engine and structure of this Cadillac Eldorado have not been altered. It has the original paintwork, wheels and chrome, too. It has, however, been adorned with all kinds of Wild West trappings.

This Suburban Cowboy, as it is called, has 18 old-fashioned rifles and revolvers, with fancy holsters and ammunition belts. The interior paneling and sills have been decorated with silver dollars – over a thousand of them.

Lowriders

Lowriders are cars that have had their bodies lowered to give a ground-hugging appearance. They are especially popular in California.

Some lowriders are fitted with a special hydraulic system to raise and lower the car at the touch of a switch. Lowriders must be raised for driving, to clear any bumps. But, when parked, they can stand with the bottom touching the ground.

▽ This 1955 Peugeot 203 is typical of a lowrider you might see in Europe. It has little modification apart from the lowering and some streamlining at the bottom. Chrome trim and wheels with chrome spokes give it a sleek look.

△ This seventies model Lincoln Continental has been given the full treatment. The theme is Hollywood, with pictures of movie stars in all kinds of places, even on the hub caps. The bodywork is painted in garish colors and the upholstery made to match.

▷ Even the inside of the trunk is upholstered.

Show cars

Show cars are made for "show" not "go." In other words, they are built for exhibition, but not for driving on the roads. Some show cars may be driven, but others are so spectacular and impractical that they have to be transported to shows.

When designing and building show cars, anything goes, but there is usually a strong theme.

△ The Space Shuttle is a simple enough theme, but it makes a spectacular looking vehicle and it can be driven.

▷ This tiny red van is so small that it is almost a toy.

▽ This is taking "big 'n' littles" to extremes, with four big rear wheels and a skinny one in front. Other features of this cross between a motorbike and an elegant old limousine are the product of a vivid imagination.

▷ This show car, "The Godfather," is based on a 1927 Ford roadster. The theme of the 1920s gangster is taken up in the display. The car itself is an extraordinary mass of gleaming, colorful machinery and bodywork.

Vans and trucks

Small vans and pick-up trucks are popular vehicles for customizing. Vans can be modified in much the same ways as cars and the extra paneling on a van gives plenty of scope for painting.

Most pick-up trucks are plain vehicles, so they provide an extra challenge for the customizer. Larger trucks are also customized.

▽ Raise a pick-up high off its wheels, add a sleek paint job and fix a bank of floodlights on the roof and you have a head-turning vehicle on the road.

▷ "Eight" seems to be the theme for this 1975 Dodge van, with its eight wheels and its eight headlights. The paint scheme and the shaping of the bodywork also add to its eye-catching appearance.

▽ This vehicle has very simple paintwork, but the "stagecoach" idea is clever. It makes an unusual delivery van.

Kit cars

Reproductions of popular models of the past and present may be bought in kit form and built by the owner.

△ A smart replica of a 1920s car.

◁ A replica of a modern Lamborghini.

▷ Sports cars of different ages made from kits – a 1950s D-Type Jaguar (above) and a 1930s Bugatti.

The story of custom cars

Custom shops

The practice, or hobby, of customizing cars began in the second half of the 1940s. Servicemen returning from the war were not satisfied with the old-fashioned cars available to them. Some owners decided to have their cars redesigned.

Special bodywork shops began to open up on the West Coast to handle this new trade. The craze spread and new magazines were published to cater to the hobby. Soon, custom shops were springing up all over the country.

△ When polished chrome came back into fashion, it was featured under the hood as well as on the bodywork.

△ An example of "shaving," the removal of chrome trim and handles.

Streamlining

At first, customizing meant streamlining. The rounded, bulky cars of the day were given a smooth, sleek look. The outside was "shaved" of all chrome fittings. These were replaced by a filler material, and the bodywork smoothed and repainted. Even door handles were removed and the doors opened by remote means. The cars were lowered as much as possible.

Custom shows

Custom car enthusiasts began to display their cars at every opportunity. Drive-in restaurants soon became popular meeting places. Then custom shows and competitions were organized, with prizes and awards. As a result, chrome became fashionable again. Lots of gleaming, polished chrome was used to catch the judges' eyes. The interiors became important, too, and some enthusiasts even

△ "Muscle cars" had powerful engines. Here, the supercharger comes through the hood.

△ The same car, a Dodge Dart, from the back. It has very wide rear "slicks," which are smooth tires.

rebuilt and upholstered the insides of the trunks.

Muscle cars

Young people eventually decided it was a waste of money to build beautiful, showy cars that often could not be used on the road. They switched their attentions to high performance cars, with big engines, four gears and strong suspension. These were called "muscle cars."

Return to customs

Government restrictions and higher insurance rates introduced in the early 1970s put an end to the muscle car era. Customizing became popular again, and it also spread to Britain and the rest of Europe.

Changing customs

Like clothes or music, custom styles are always changing. Street rodding – rebuilding pre-1949 cars – has a large following. Lowriding is also popular.

△ Admirers study a street rod as it cruises around a drive-in restaurant.

Facts and records

△ An extreme example of chopping. This Austin Mini, a British economy car, is claimed to be the world's lowest road-legal car. It stands only 34.5 in (88 cm) high.

Chopping

Lowering a car's roof, or chopping, involves cutting down the door pillars, welding them back to the roof and shortening the windows. It is easier to do this on cars with an upright structure.

The driver often has to sit in a hunched-forward position when a car's roof has been chopped, as there is very little headroom.

Cut 'n' shut

The practice of changing the length of a car is called "cut 'n' shut." If a car is to be lengthened, it is first "cut," then a section is added and finally it is closed up again, or "shut." A car may be shortened in a similar way, with a section removed between the "cut" and the "shut."

△ A car elongated by means of "cut 'n' shut." This 1967 Cadillac has been "stretched" to a world record 48 ft (14.6 m) and has 10 wheels.

△ Another example of "cut 'n' shut," a shortened Chevelle.

△ Under the hood of the same Chevelle, with a toy animal to match the paintwork.

Glossary

Big 'n' littles
A combination of large tires at the rear and small ones in front.

Chrome
The metallic fittings on a car, such as bumpers, door handles and trim.

Cruise
A display in which custom cars are driven slowly around the streets or perhaps a drive-in restaurant to show them off.

Custom car
A car altered to change its appearance from the factory model.

Flamed paintwork
A wavy paintwork pattern that looks like flames.

Frenched
Recessed into the bodywork.

Kit car
A car made from a kit supplied by the manufacturer.

Lakes pipes
Thin chrome pipes that run along the side of a car at the bottom to give it a more streamlined appearance.

Lowrider
A car that has had its body very much lowered.

Muscle car
High-powered car popular in the 1960s.

Replica
A copy of a past model made with new parts.

Shaving
Taking off chrome trim and other hardware and giving the car a completely smooth appearance.

Show car
A car built purely for show and not for driving on the roads.

Streamlining
Giving a car a smooth, sleek appearance.

Street rod
A custom car based on a model built before 1949.

Stretched
Lengthened – either the whole car or a part of it.

Supercharger
A part used to pump extra air and fuel into an engine.

Index

big 'n' littles 12, 21, 31
bodywork 13, 19, 22, 25, 28
Bugatti 27

Cadillac 17, 30
carburetor 9
chassis 6, 10
Chevelle 30
chopped roof 9, 10, 13, 30
chrome 7, 8, 9, 13, 17, 18, 28, 31
Citroën 14
Corsair 26
cruise 10, 31
custom car 6, 7, 13, 31
custom shop 28
custom show 28
cut 'n' shut 30

Dodge 25, 29
drive-in 28, 29

engine 6, 7, 11, 13, 17, 29

flamed paintwork 6, 8, 31
floodlights 24
Ford 12, 22
frenched 8, 31

grille 9, 15

headlights 9, 28
hood 28, 30
hub caps 8, 19

interior 6, 7, 13, 16, 17

Jaguar 27

kit car 7, 26, 27, 31

Lakes pipes 13, 31
Lamborghini 26
Lincoln 19
low 'n' lean look 9
lowrider 7, 18, 19, 29, 31

muscle car 29, 31

paintwork 6, 15, 17, 25
Peugeot 17
pick-up truck 24
Plymouth 10

replica 26, 31

shaving 8, 28, 31
show car 7, 20, 21, 22, 31
streamlining 18, 28, 31
street rod 6, 7, 9, 11, 12, 29, 31
stretched 30, 31
supercharger 29, 31
suspension 9, 10, 29

theme 13, 20, 22
tires 8, 10, 11, 29
trunk 19, 29

van 21, 24, 25
VW 14–15

wheels 9, 12, 17, 18